A Note to Parents and Teachers

DK READERS is a compelling reading programme for children. The programme is designed in conjunction with leading literacy experts, including Cliff Moon M.Ed., who has spent many years as a teacher and teacher educator specializing in reading. Cliff Moon has written more than 160 books for children and teachers. He is series editor to Collins Big Cat.

Beautiful illustrations and superb full-colour photographs combine with engaging, easy-to-read stories to offer a fresh approach to each subject in the series. Each DK READER is guaranteed to capture a child's interest while developing his or her reading skills, general knowledge, and love of reading.

The five levels of DK READERS are aimed at different reading abilities, enabling you to choose the books that are exactly right for your child:

Pre-level 1: Learning to read
Level 1: Beginning to read
Level 2: Beginning to read alone
Level 3: Reading alone
Level 4: Proficient readers

The "normal" age at which a child begins to read can be anywhere from three to eight years old. Adult participation through the lower levels is very helpful for providing encouragement, discussing storylines and sounding out unfamiliar words.

No matter which level you select, you can be sure that you are helping your child read, ther read to

DK

LONDON, NEW YORK, MUNICH,
MELBOURNE, AND DELHI

Project Editor Louise Pritchard
Art Editor Jill Plank
Production Siu Chan
Picture Researcher Liz Moore
Illustrator Peter Dennis
Jacket Designer Natalie Godwin
Publishing Manager Bridget Giles

Reading Consultant
Cliff Moon, M.Ed.

Published in Great Britain by
Dorling Kindersley Limited
80 Strand, London WC2R 0RL

Copyright © 2010 Dorling Kindersley Limited
A Penguin Company

4 6 8 10 9 7 5 3
008-177254-Mar/2010

A CIP catalogue record for this book
is available from the British Library

ISBN: 978-1-40535-250-5

Colour reproduction by Colourscan, Singapore
Printed and bound in China by L. Rex Printing Co. Ltd.

The publisher would like to thank the following for
their kind permission to reproduce their photographs:
Key: c=centre; t=top; b=bottom; l=left; r=right
National Geographic Image Collection: Chris Johns 26–27b; **NOAA
Photo Library/NOAA Central Library** (www.photolib.noaa.gov/: 28t, 30;
Planet Earth Pictures: Alex Benwell 15br, Paolo Fanciulli 7br; **Robert
Harding Picture Library**: 16, Sheila Beougher 18bl, Warren Faidley/
Agliolo 1br, Warren Faidley/Int'l Stock 16–17, 18tr, Jeff Greenberg 22tr;
Tony Stone Images: 21tr, Christoph Burki 5tr, Jerry Kobalenko 4–5, John
Lund 32, Alan R Moller 19b, Camille Tokerud 15cr;
Topham Picturepoint: 25br, J. McTyre 24.
Jacket images: *Front*: **Getty Images**: Paul & Lindamarie Ambrose

All other images © Dorling Kindersley
For further information see: www.dkimages.com

Discover more at
www.dk.com

DK READERS

Twisters!

Written by Kate Hayden

A Dorling Kindersley Book

Rob was working
in his farmyard in Texas.
It was a peaceful spring day but
his dog, Barney, was unhappy.
He hid under a tractor and
would not come out.
Rob wondered if Barney was ill.

Second sense

Animals have sharper senses than we have. Many can sense changes in the weather, like just before a bad storm.

Suddenly the sky went dark.
Hailstones as big as golf balls
pelted down from the sky.
Thunder rolled and
lightning flashed.
A few moments later
there was a deathly stillness.
Somehow, Barney had known!

As Bob looked on,
huge black clouds began to spin.
They bubbled at the top
like boiling milk.
Gusts of wind blew straw around.
Just then, a finger of cloud
spiralled down from the sky.
A twister!

Rob stood rooted to the spot.

The twister touched the ground.

Mud and grass swirled up

like smoke from a bonfire.

That was only the start of it.

The twister began to move.

It skipped and bounced

across the fields.

It grew bigger, faster and dirtier

as it picked up mud

from the ground.

Waterspouts
Twisters out at sea
are called waterspouts.
They whisk up water.
The tallest one seen
was 1.6 km (1 mile) tall.

Rob watched in horror
as the twister went
towards his neighbour's farm.
It picked up straw, trees –
and even a farm truck.
It spun them around in its funnel.
Rob sighed with relief when
the twister moved away.
He thought he was safe.
But then the twister
changed direction –
straight towards him!

Suddenly the twister was hanging
right over Rob's farm.
There was a noise
like a rushing waterfall,
then – BANG!
The barn exploded
as if a bomb had gone off inside it.

Rob ran with Barney
to the cellar in his house.
His ears were hurting and
he could hardly breathe.
That's because the air pressure
inside a twister is very low.
This makes people's ears ache and
causes buildings to explode.

Just as Rob reached
the cellar,
his front porch flew off
with an ear-splitting CRASH!
Then came a SMASH
as the house windows blew in.
Two minutes later, all was silent.

Rob came up from the cellar.
Furniture lay smashed on the floor.
Most of the doors and
windows were gone.
Rob felt lucky
to be alive.

Friends helped Rob to clean up.
They lived nearby but
their house wasn't touched.

Warm air

Cold air

Twisters can form
when cold air meets warm air.
The warm air is sucked up
in a swirling column
called a funnel cloud.
It spins at great speed.
Twisters contain
the most deadly winds
in the world.

No-one knows
what a twister will do next.
It can lift up a large truck and
smash it to pieces, but
leave small objects undamaged.
One twister picked up a baby
and set him down safely
90 metres (300 feet)
away.
The baby did not
even wake up!

Strange showers
When twisters drop
things they've picked up,
strange things can happen.
A twister in England
caused a shower of frogs.

There are lots of strange stories about twisters. A twister once blew away a man's birth certificate. The twister carried it 80 kilometres (50 miles) then dropped it in a friend's garden. One twister sucked up some roses and water from a vase. It dropped them in another room but it left the vase on the table.

Another twister picked up
a jar of pickles and carried
the jar for kilometres (miles)
without damaging it.

Twisters come in many different shapes and sizes. They can be thin, white and wispy. Or they can be big, thick and black.

They can even be red or green! If a twister travels across a muddy field, the mud turns it brown – and very smelly!

Twisters can grow bigger and faster
as they go along.
Some look as if they have
a loop or knot in the middle.
Some are wider at the bottom
than at the top.
Some are shaped like a tube and
others look like a slice of pie.

Lots of people
have seen a twister
from the outside.
But only a few have looked
inside a twister and survived.

A farmer named Will Keller
once looked up into a twister
from his underground shelter.
Just as he closed
the door of his shelter,
he saw lots of mini twisters
inside the big twister.
These mini twisters can rip
through a building and
slice it to shreds.

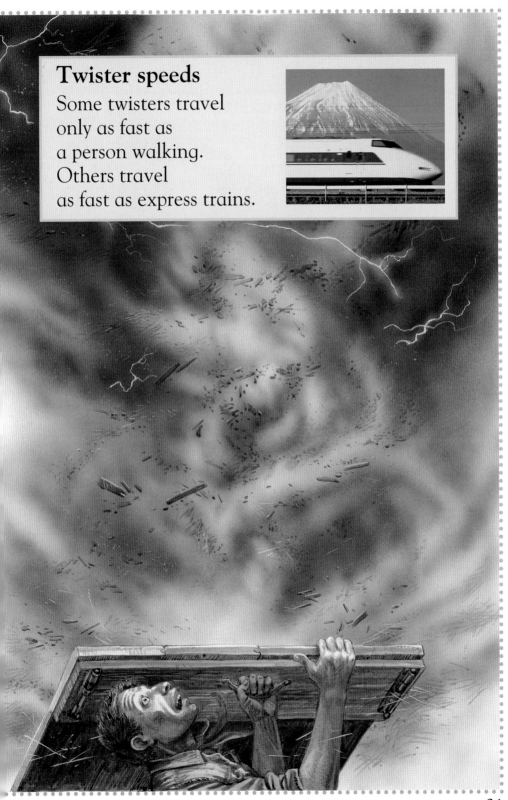

Twister speeds

Some twisters travel
only as fast as
a person walking.
Others travel
as fast as express trains.

21

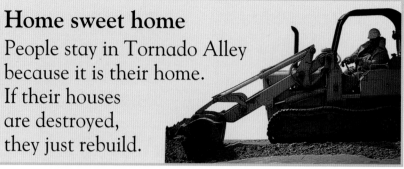

Home sweet home
People stay in Tornado Alley because it is their home. If their houses are destroyed, they just rebuild.

Twisters are also known as tornados. There is an area in the USA that is called Tornado Alley. It is famous for its deadly twisters. Up to 300 occur there every year between April and July. They kill more than 80 people.

Twisters form during these months
as warm air from the south meets
cold air from the north –
right over Tornado Alley.

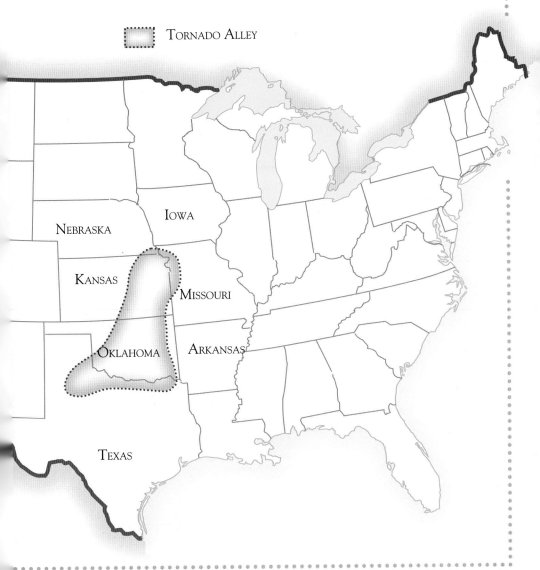

TORNADO ALLEY

NEBRASKA

IOWA

KANSAS

MISSOURI

OKLAHOMA   ARKANSAS

TEXAS

Twisters are graded from 0 to 5 on a scale called the Fujita Scale. An F0 damages chimneys. An F1 snaps telephone poles. An F2 rips off roofs. An F3 turns over trains. An F4 destroys even strong homes. An F5 leaves few things standing. In 1999, an F5 ripped through Oklahoma City, Oklahoma. It killed 45 people.

The worst twister
In 1925, one twister in Tornado Alley destroyed four towns in less than four hours. It killed 689 people.

People in Tornado Alley are
well prepared for twisters.
Most of them have
an underground shelter
outside their home.

Emergency supplies
People keep
emergency supplies
in their shelters –
food, drink, torches
and a first-aid kit.

Some people in Texas have
a fibreglass shelter
buried in their back garden.

People without
a shelter hide
in a cellar
or small room
in the middle
of their house.

*The Malone family
next to their
fibreglass shelter
before it is buried*

Gary England is
a TV weather reporter
in Oklahoma City.
When lots of twisters
are expected,
Gary's team stays on the air
for 30 hours or more.

Scientists tell Gary what
the weather will be like.
Gary can then tell viewers.
The scientists use a computer
to help them forecast twisters.
The computer makes a picture
that shows where a twister is
and how fast it is travelling.

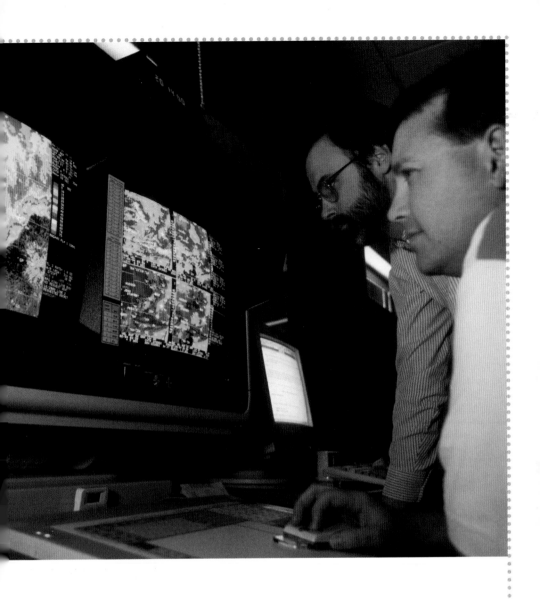

Forecasts from space

Spacecraft called satellites
orbit around Earth.
Some send information
about the weather
to scientists on Earth.

The scientists can tell Gary
what they think will happen.
But storm trackers on the road
know what is actually happening.
These people risk their lives
to find and follow twisters.
Many of them have
modern equipment
such as a satellite dish.

The trackers tell Gary
all about a twister –
where it is and
where it is going.
They can even tell him
when a twister is brewing.

In the past, people did not know when a twister was coming. Today, the trackers and scientists give people time to find shelter, and hundreds of lives are saved.

A storm tracker's modern truck

Twister facts

People in Tornado Alley
can check for twisters
when they fill their cars
with petrol.
Many pumps show
the weather forecast
on a screen.

Winds inside a twister
can spin around
at nearly
500 km (310 miles) per hour.

In April 1974,
148 tornados tore through
13 states in the USA.
Six of them were F5s –
the strongest type of tornado.

In 1994, in Australia,
hundreds of fish fell
from the sky.
This was probably
the work of a twister.

Twisters that suck up
sand in deserts
are called dust devils.

A twister can last
for any length of time –
from a few minutes
to an hour.